REVIEWS OF OTHER BOOKS BY MOLLIE BARTELT

A Simple Guide to Saving Your Family Photos

The step-by-step guidelines provided in this book are clearly thought out and you can tell is based on the author's experience of doing lots of photo organizing. Having made a couple of attempts to organize my family's photos I identify with why Bartelt doesn't call the process easy. However, after reading through this guide I definitely feel like I now have a simple road map to follow that can finally get me on my way to getting my photo organizing project completed. – R. Lippert

If you've inherited family photos or you just want to get your own photos organized and digitized, this book is for you. It is well written and easy to read. It provides advice on many different scenarios (family photos, a professional photographer's collection, etc.). As well, the book explains how to incorporate physical photos and digital photos into one organized collection. – Jacki Hollywood Browne, Unclutter.com

Right now, there are about 3,000 pictures on my phone and around 30,000 sitting every which place around my house. No joke, I thought this book was going to be 250 pages, how do you cram all your family life? But this is an easy quick read and super well organized. Bullet points and simple steps. I am excited to pull some tips out and apply them in my own life. – Gina E.

Family photos as a great parenting tool? Yes! This book gives the strategies and encouragement you'll need to use those pictures you've snapped through the years. Feel great about your memories and strengthen your relationships at the same time." – Deborah Gilboa, MD, author of Get the Behavior You Want... Without Being the Parent You Hate!

The Pixologist's Guide to Creating a Memorable Photo Book

"What a wonderful 'how-to' guide! This book is a terrific resource for the DIY family memory-keeper and you have it organized in a very logical, easy to follow format. You also give the readers tons of great resources to choose from as well as some creative ideas to get their projects started. I highly recommend this book to anyone who needs help learning the ins and outs of creating meaningful photo books." – Donna P.

This book is a "must-read" for anyone who enjoys preserving stories! With plenty of inspiration and resources to help you get started, Mollie outlines all the basics you need to know when making your own photo books! I highly recommend it! – Caroline Guntur, The Swedish Organizer

If you need photo book help, this book has a lot to offer. With simple language and clear steps, I found it easy to follow the system to make a photo book. There are many options and examples to explore and this guide has so much in one place. Plus, I grew up in the late 80s and early 90s and could identify with the author's reminiscing of the way printing used to work.
– Mary

BOOKS BY MOLLIE BARTELT

Available on Amazon.com
A Simple Guide to Saving Your Family Photos
A Simple Guide to Tackling Your Digital Photo Mess

Books Available Through HenschelHaus Books and Amazon.com
The Pixologist's Guide to Organizing and Preserving Your Family Photos
The Pixologist's Guide to Creating a Memorable Photo Book

HenschelHaus Books: https://henschelhausbooks.com

A Simple Guide to Creating a Photo Estate

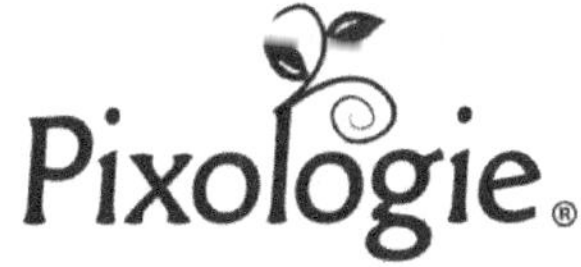

For permission requests, please contact:

Pixologie
9803 S. 13th Street
Oak Creek, WI 53154
mollieb@pixologieinc.com

ISBN: 978-1-948326-15-5
LCCN: 2020900806

A Simple Guide to Creating a Photo Estate

By Mollie Bartelt

Co-Founder of Pixologie

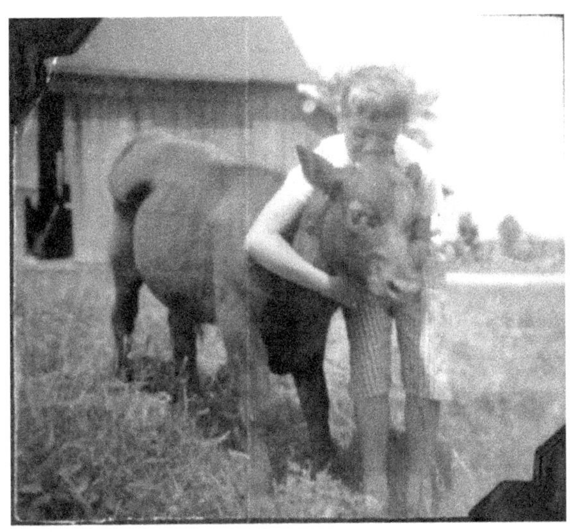

INTRODUCTION

When you are gone, what will be remembered of your life? How will your stories be told? What legacy do you want to leave behind?

As a professional photo organizer, I can help you with these questions. My friend and business partner, Ann Matuszak, and I have organized over 1 million photos (which includes prints, negatives, slides, memorabilia, film and video) for our clients. Legacies and stories include:

- Family milestones – From births to graduations, weddings and death, the circle of life turns very fast. Our clients tell us how meaningful it is to see photos and be reminded of the memories.

- Fascinating accounts - Our parents experienced growing up in a world without technology. Our grandparents grew up, most likely, without television and our great-grandparents may not even have had electricity. We marvel at photos showing what life was like, not that long ago. Watching reel to reel film with no sound still brings people to tears when they see their long-gone relatives once again.

- Work ethic – From settling the country to farming in the 1800s and through the Depression, our ancestors had to work hard to live. We've seen photos of grit, determination, poverty, joy and appreciation of a simpler life.

- Service to our country - Members of client families have served from before the United States was even founded. We have preserved photos and documents from the Civil War through modern day service.

- Family traditions – First communions, bar mitzvahs, gardening, outdoor life, past times and countless other traditions are important to preserve. Our clients hold dear memories of apple picking, sharing holiday meals together, celebrating religious milestones, baking special recipes and so much more.

- Community growth – The place you grew up in didn't always look like it did then, and it certainly doesn't look the same today. In one instance, we scanned photos of landscapes where there was just the start of a town. Seventy years later, today, the town is a bustling city of over 100,000 people.

If you are a politician, famous actor/actress, CEO of some large company, or somehow famous in your own way, other people may help tell your story and preserve your legacy. From biographies to endowments and other memorials, there are a good number of ways for a person to not be forgotten after they are gone. Indeed, one of our clients led an outstanding academic career and was blessed to have a building named after him.

But for most of us, we'll have to figure how to pass our legacy on to future generations. Let's go back to those questions:

- When you are gone, what will be remembered of your life?
- How will your stories be told?
- What legacy do you want to leave behind?

Can you believe some of the answers are in your photo collection? Sound crazy? It might – if you are like a lot of our clients and your photo collection is a mess of photos in too many places to count! At our company, Pixologie, Ann and I have worked with countless people in taming their photo collections.

Using our photo organizing system, we've been able to provide a simple way to sort and save the most important memories our clients have. We've seen a lot of messy photo collections! Ann considers your photo collection your most important, neglected asset. Because we've seen the power of memories at work, we call our final desired outcome, a photo estate.

Creating a photo estate may help you answer all of these questions. In this book, I'll explain how a photo estate can be a treasure for future generations. I'll also talk about how you can create your own photo estate with some easy steps. You'll see a few examples of a photo estate, from small to large. And, if all else fails, I will touch upon how you can get help for your photo estate project.

We are thrilled you want to learn more about ensuring your history, stories and legacy are preserved for future generations. We hope you are reading this book to create your own photo estate.

If you have inherited a photo collection from a parent or other relative who has died, this book will walk you through how to preserve that person's legacy as well.

Thank you so much for joining Ann and I on this journey to preserving family legacies for generations to come.

CHAPTER 1 – WHAT IS A PHOTO ESTATE?

Before we started working with people's photo collections, the term photo estate wasn't even a concept. But think about it. When there's a fire, what do you think instantly after getting family to safety? Most people agree, "Grab the photos."

Back in the 1970s, 1980s and 1990s, it was easier to "grab the photos." Consumers were used to the flow of preserving memories. It went something like this:

- Buy film, put it in the camera
- Take your pictures
- Take film to be developed
- Pick up envelopes of pictures
- Buy a photo album and put the pictures in it

Sometimes, the last step was skipped, and the envelopes of pictures ended up in a box, drawer or bin. I've worked with clients whose five photo albums contained all of the family photos. And, I've met clients who've had 50 photo albums. In the event of a fire, this last client would have had a tough time picking which albums to grab first. For those who had the envelopes without albums, they also would have had a hard time gathering up the pictures if disaster hit.

Imagine you are living in the 1970s, 1980s or 1990s. Which statements are true?

- My five photo albums are my photo estate
- My fifty-five photo albums are my photo estate
- My photo envelopes in boxes, drawers and bins are my photo estate

Well, maybe, I should share our definition of a photo estate before you choose which statements are true. A photo estate is:

A collection of photos, film, video, documents and memorabilia organized in a manner that allows another person or persons to view the photos, learn about the lives documented, and be impacted by the legacy of those people.

Now, take a look at the statements again. Which are true based on our definition? If you answered true to the first two statements, you are correct . . . *if we are still imagining we are in the 1970s, 1980s and 1990s.*

Today, we are the beneficiaries of a technological and digital revolution over the past twenty years. Now, a photo estate most likely will be digital, the easiest format to maintain, share and pass on to future generations. The digital photo estate can be supplemented with wonderful printed books to have on the coffee table and to share with family members.

Background of an Estate

Most commonly, people consider the word "estate" to relate to the net worth of a person including all of their financial assets, land and possessions. Many careers are centered around helping people with financial planning; and with the goal of leaving a financial legacy behind for their heirs.

We've spoken with a variety of people in these careers from life insurance agents to financial planners to estate attorneys and more. You might be surprised at a common occurrence that seems to cross all of these areas. We've received general agreement that:

75% of people who inherit a sum of money spend their inheritance in less than two years.

In the past, families worked hard to accumulate wealth. Then they lived off interest payments from the principal.

Today, inheritances can be spent on home remodeling, vacations, debt payoff and many other big-ticket items. All the advance planning a person can do goes up in smoke less than two years after he or she has died.

Can you imagine your financial legacy being gone in such a short time? What about leaving a different kind of legacy? A legacy that can be found in a photo estate - where the net worth of our lives is collected, preserved and passed on to future generations?

Let's break down the definition of a photo estate.

A Collection

The first part of our definition includes *"a collection of photos, film, video, documents and memorabilia."* You can see that we include much more than photos in our definition. Always, when we organize a client's photos, we find one or more of the following:

- Slides
- Negatives
- Reels of film
- Video tapes
- Holiday photo cards
- Regular cards and letters
- Certificates
- Documents
- ID Cards, report cards, diaries
- Many other types of memorabilia

> **For simpler reading, consider the word "photos" to mean all of the items in this list.**

All of these items may help tell the story of someone's life. And, all of these items can be scanned and preserved along with the pictures. However, just because they can all be scanned (as well as every photo ever taken), we must organize, or curate, these items. There is no sense in making a digital mess of a physical mess.

We find that only a small percentage of all of your photo collection actually needs to be preserved. Let's talk about the next part of our photo estate definition.

Organized in a Manner

The next part of our definition is, *"organized in a manner...."* Most everyone we meet has a photo collection. However, very few people actually have their photos organized. Those with photo albums have a head start on organizing, but the albums may be creating other issues.

Back in the day when we used photo albums, people tended to save every photo taken. Even if the photo was a bad picture. Rolls of film only contained 24 pictures per roll, so people often saved all the photos. So, these photo albums, which could hold up to 600 photos, sometimes are not very fun to look at. Here are the drawbacks of preserving all photos in albums or even the albums themselves:

- Photo albums contain bad pictures that don't need to be saved

- You won't want to save all the repetitive photos (i.e. gift openings at parties, different angles of the family garden, etc.)
- Albums are not photo safe, discoloring and damaging the photos
- Nobody wants to inherit a bunch of old, mismatched albums
- Photo albums are clunky to haul around. And they are at risk to be lost in a move, a fire, to time or other disaster

Many people today simply use their smartphone to take photos. In a different way, we all have a head start on having photos organized chronologically. However, chances are great, you have digital photos in many different places. Here are the drawbacks of a digital collection of photos on your phone.

- Missing all the digital photos from your other devices (unless you are the rare person that has all your photos in one place – a mystically state of something I refer to as photo nirvana!)
- Many, many repetitive photos that need to be deleted because we can now take 50 photos in less than a minute.
- Photos taken for information purposes that would be embarrassing or unsafe to share with other people mixed in your collection
- Difficult to do things with those photos (unless you have found that right app and/or website and have tech skills to

share your collection easily, make photo books, prints and more right from your phone.)

- Little to no ability or capability to pass this collection on to the next generation.

Besides photo albums and smartphones, photos are saved in countless other places. You can just see how difficult it would be for your photo collection to be passed on to future generations in its current state of existence.

So, this second part of the definition, *organized in a manner,* really is where the crux of creating a photo estate lies. It is essentially "curating" your current photo collection. We must find those most important photos and other media that are key to preserving your family's story.

A photo estate does not have to be huge . . . in fact, less than 100 photos might do the trick. For some people, the photo estate may contain hundreds of photos. Most of our clients have thousands of photos and other items preserved. Your photo estate could contain:

- Photos of parents, grandparents & great-grandparents, perhaps a couple of where they lived, young and old, wedding

- Photos of your growing up years

- A few photos from each year of your adult, career and family life - capturing what was important to you and what you'd like to see people in the future know about and perhaps be inspired by

- Photos that show your traditions (religious milestones, holiday celebrations, cultural events, etc.)
- Pictures of the places you lived and a few of the places you traveled (with significant landmarks)
- Any other pictures that have special meaning to you

View the Photos

This part of our definition, *"that allows another person or persons to view the photos,"* offers how people will view your photos. What does this mean? Essentially, your photo estate will need to be accessible by family, descendants and, if desired, other people who may have an interest.

Let's talk about how the photos might be viewed. Each of our clients have had a different set of skills, interests and desires for how they want to view their photos. Always, the printed photos must be digitized to be future safe.

Here are some of the solutions we have provided:

- Digitized photos organized chronologically and provided back to the client on USB drives
- Organized photo libraries copied to computers using a variety of photo software
- A permanent online family photo archive
- Family history photo books with printed copies to share as well as a digital copy accessible online

With the first two solutions, the ability for others to view the collection may be more difficult. Passing the digital file folders presents risks related to the heirs depending upon their skills, computer software and motivation to preserve the digital files. The third option provides current shareable access to the entire estate. The final point gives your family a tangible summary or highlight that is not technology dependent.

Your choice in how the photo estate is viewed is critical to ensuring future generations can benefit from your work now and the legacy you will leave. We'll go into much further detail on this.

Learn About the Lives Documented

The next part of our definition is *"learn about the lives documented."* This point clearly separates most photo collections (or photo messes) from a photo estate. What in our lives could future generations learn from our photos? Consider these points:

- In our lifetime, we have witnessed unprecedented technological and digital revolution. Future generations should know what life was like before we had everything at our fingertips
- Hard labor and strong work ethic are the foundation of our country and of our families; but these traits are not celebrated
- Trends in society appear to be decreased honoring of traditions, decreased religious involvement, and increased depression and suicide

I can only imagine what the next 50 years will bring.

Dr. Robyn Fivush started the Family Narratives Lab to study how memories influence childhood coping and more. From their website, "Her work focuses on early memory with an emphasis on the social construction of autobiographical memory and the relations among memory, narrative, trauma and coping."[1]

She and her research team believe that "Family reminiscing creates a shared history and helps to maintain emotional bonds." In a recent article for Psychology Today, Dr. Fivush, stated,

> *"research from The Family Narratives Lab showing that children and adolescents who know more of their family stories show higher well-being on multiple measures, including higher self-esteem, higher academic competence, higher social competence, and fewer behavior problems."[2]*

Fivush points out that the historical questions aren't the important part of this exercise. Instead, it is the family discussions that come from starting the conversation.

First Things First, a non-profit that focuses on strengthening family relationships, writes:

> *"So, the next time your children roll their eyes during a story from the past, just remember that you are building what Duke and Fivush call "the child's intergenerational self." But that's not all. You're also increasing their personal strength and giving them moral guidance."[3]*

It is important to note that Dr. Fivush's research does not pertain to including photos in the discussion, but I believe that photos help spur the conversation.

Now, the last word of this part of our definition, *"documented."* Yes, there needs to be documentation.

Case in point: You may have photos from the 1920s or earlier in your collection. Do you know the people in the pictures? Do you know where the photos were taken?

We want our photo estates to explain to future generations about our lives today. Documentation is required. Today, we might know who is in a photo and what is happening. One hundred years from now, will the person looking at the picture know these details? No, unless the photo has documentation.

Documentation can take the form of:

- Scanned backsides of photos with handwritten notes
- Metadata (digital information) added to a scanned photo
- Captions and narratives in a photo book

I will be addressing how to add documentation to photos later in this book.

Be Impacted by the Legacy

This part of our definition, *"be impacted by the legacy of those people"* brings people to tears often at our studio. When you see your memories come back to life in an organized manner, you can't help but be moved.

We've seen many a client grabbing for a tissue when they look at scanned slides of their long-gone grandparents. Or, when reel to reel film has been digitized, a client watching his young wife running around on the grass in front of the house with their son. Our clients are impacted.

As I consider my photo estate, I choke up looking at a picture of my sister when she was 8 years old wearing a Children's Hospital t-shirt after recent surgery looking at a carnation, taken in 1982.

The year 2009 was a challenging year for my family financially. I felt terrible that we couldn't do much with the kids to have an enjoyable summer. When I look at the photos taken during that time, I found peace seeing that we actually had many free adventures that summer. If I didn't have the photos, I wouldn't have remembered that we provided fun and a happy environment without much expense.

Photos impact people. Your photo estate **will** move you, inspire you and provide you with the reminder of good memories, many forgotten.

Your photo estate **will** move future generations. I don't know what stories, traditions and legacy you have. Please don't think it doesn't matter to save your pictures. Your heirs and future generations will be impacted by your photos in the following ways:

- Your family history will be treated as something of value, a treasure to be preserved, a source of pride and will be looked upon with love and appreciation.
- They will have a connection to you in some way. It may be facial resemblances, a valued tradition continued, similar career pursued or another shared trait.

- They may have DNA results that connect them to people they don't know. Your photos and documentation can provide clues to their ancestors filling in genealogy gaps.

- Your stories may become family legends that help provide fun reminiscences about the personalities and exploits of the family. I've got a few in my family!

Now, just because you go through the effort of creating a photo estate, don't assume everyone will be thrilled immediately and want to look through it with joy, excitement and anticipation. Don't assume that everyone to come after you will eagerly look through your photo estate and experience all of these points.

Don't assume everyone will be thrilled with your photo estate. It may take years for this treasure to be fully appreciated.

You'll want to take the personal satisfaction of completing your photo estate as your main reward.

Sometimes, it takes time for others to appreciate the work done on creating a photo estate. For some family members, there is no desire to look upon the past and revisit forgotten memories. Reasons for this include:

- Some people truly don't feel a connection to old photos or want to reminisce.

- Some have no interest in talking about family history.

- A person could have experienced emotional trauma (childhood abuse or even a recent death) and the photos would trigger forgotten feelings and sadness.

I have this situation in my family and every time I try to talk about looking at family photos, I have caused my family member to feel upset, guilty and depressed. Fortunately, she is willing to look at a photo here and there to let me know who is in the picture. I treasure those moments.

If you experience a lack of interest from your family, focus on sharing your photo estate with the people who want to be involved. And remember, generations from now, there will be family members who will be delighted to look through your photos. They will talk about the stories of what came before and enjoy discovering their history together.

Okay, we have definitely picked apart the definition of a photo estate. Now it's time to learn how to bring it all together.

Notes

1 - Family Narratives Lab -

https://scholarblogs.emory.edu/familynarrativeslab/people/

2 - https://www.psychologytoday.com/us/blog/the-stories-our-lives/201611/the-do-you-know-20-questions-about-family-stories

3 - https://firstthings.org/teaching-family-history

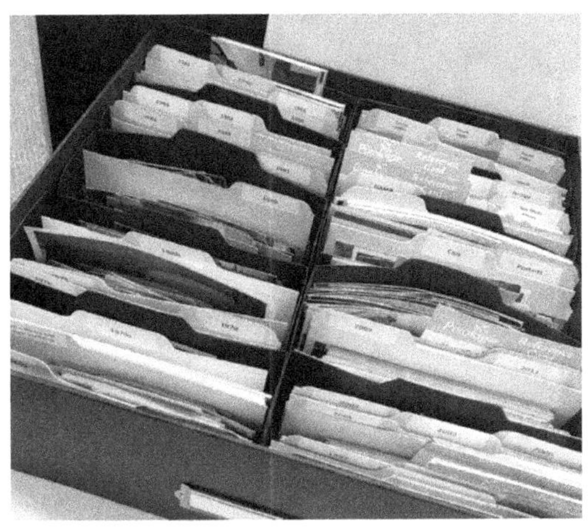

CHAPTER 2 – CHOOSE AN ORGANIZING METHOD

Overwhelmed by your photos? You are not alone. In previous books and at many community presentations, I have taught my system on how to organize family photo collections. Over the years, I have heard many people express appreciation for the system. And, indeed, I've been contacted by some men and women who have followed the system and successfully organized every last photo they had. It's simple, but it can take a long period of time.

But for the vast majority of readers, I believe they are struggling with decades of accumulated photos including collections inherited from other family members and a digital mess of photos.

Due to time and the demands of daily life, a good size photo collection can take someone years to fully organize and preserve the best photos. And, most people never finish. I've seen the evidence of numerous organizing attempts when I meet new clients.

In this chapter, I will share my original method (or full method) for organizing photos for those of you that wish to completely tackle your photo mess. But for those of you who would like to focus on the most important photos, I offer an alternate, the shortcut method.

Read through both and determine which one fits your needs, time frame and intended outcome.

Completely Tackle Your Photo Mess – Full Method

With this Full Method, I'm sharing the steps detailed in *"The Pixologist's Guide to Organizing and Preserving Your Family Photos."* Please check that book out as it provides many more examples, photos, tips and tools than I can cover in this book.

In a quick nutshell, here are the overall steps:

1. Bring all your photos to one place
2. Sort all photos by major category
3. Break down each major category's photos into subcategories
4. Fine tune subcategories as desired

As you can see, you will be sorting through your photos in phases. It is possible you'll be handling your photos anywhere from two to four or more times, depending on your organizing style. Whenever possible, throw away photos that are duplicates, bad pictures, repetitive in nature, etc. You will appreciate having less to sort in the final step of organization.

Once you have sorted and organized your photos into their final place, you will want to scan them.

Step One - Bring It All Together

Your first step will be to collect your photos into one place. Even if you are not starting right away, bringing all the photos together is a great beginning and a great feeling. Just start a table or a room and begin moving your boxes and albums there.

Why bring it all together?

- Seeing your photos all together helps provide perspective on what needs to be completed.
- Treating this project as an "all or nothing" venture provides you with a clear goal.
- Identifying and tossing duplicates become much easier.
- Enjoying the final organization is much more satisfying knowing you got through it all!

Visit www.pixologieinc.com/tools to download a Photo Inventory form. It will help you find all the places your photos might be hiding. I've included this form in the Appendix D at the end of this book.

Slides & Negatives

As you are bringing your photos together, you may find negatives and slides. We include these in our photo organization projects but handle them separately from the photos.

Do you have negatives still stored in envelopes? You can toss them if you know for sure you have the photos. If the negatives are not with their photos and you are unsure if you have the photos, place the negatives in a bin and set to the side. Leave the negatives in their envelope and any documentation, if possible.

If you have slides, chances are there are hundreds or thousands of them. There is ample opportunity to discard slides from landscape scenes to repetitive photos and more. Find a lightboard, projector or slide viewer to help determine which ones to keep.

Negatives and slides can be more costly to digitize. Spending time figuring out which ones are keepers is a good investment of time.

Group your slides and negatives by date or category. Scan them yourself with a consumer grade scanner or hire a professional to scan them.

Film & Video

You may also find reels of film and video that needs preserving. Generally, reels of film will be of good quality and content, depending upon the film used and the skill of the film camera operator. You can expect to pay between 50 cents and a $1.00 per foot of film. This can also become costly, given that one three-inch reel of film holds 50 feet and a seven-inch reel holds 400 feet.

Video tapes vary in quality and generally contain long clips. You may have VHS, VHS-C, MiniDV or 8mm tapes. Sometimes, the tapes contain a lot of repetitive content of kids' sports games, concerts, family reunions and more. However, you can find real gem portions of video that help tell your family story. Tape transfer costs anywhere from $12 to $90 and higher per tape depending upon location, quality desired and format returned.

There are software packages that allow you to transfer your own videos if you have the right equipment. If not, you'll need to find a provider to transfer the videos. Film requires finding a provider to digitize the reels.

With film and video, you'll want to consider the costs to converting them safely. You can find a balance with knowing how important good clips are to your photo estate. Seeing people moving, interacting with one another, smiling and alive makes the expense worthwhile. Our clients love seeing the video and film we've digitized. At least half the time, tissues are needed!

Tips on Tossing Photos

Our goal with photo organization and creating a photo estate is NOT to save every moment ever captured on film. Rather, we want to save photos that provide us with the essence of what life was like.

My "what to save" recommendations refer to any type of photo collection whether printed or digital. I have found that sometimes bad photos are the most precious to keep. So, with that being said, please use your heart and your judgment in determining what you want to save. You don't have to save the following types of pictures:

1. Landscape photos of most kinds. If there's no family, you probably don't need it.

2. Crowd settings where no one is recognizable and school activity photos where you cannot see your children

3. Nearly every zoo animal photo ever taken (although I do have a photo of Sampson, the famous gorilla at the Milwaukee County Zoo when I was growing up)

4. Event photos like birthday parties and Christmas – eliminate all the repetitive photos of opening gifts and other activities

5. Unflattering photos – this doesn't mean throw away every photo of yourself! Be smart and kind – remember, the photo estate is more than about your view of yourself!

6. Poor quality photos, pictures of floors, ceilings, blank, black or blurry photos.

7. Any others that serve no value to your legacy

As a guide, you'll want to save 8-10 photos from most any event showing the best moments, who was there and what was happening. If you choose to save more, that is perfectly fine – I provide the number just as a reference.

For vacation and travel photos, you may wish to save more if this is your photo estate project. However, if you are working on a deceased parent's photo estate, you probably don't need to save as many of the vacation and travel photos.

Case in point: I had the amazing fortune to travel to Spain last year. I took over 1200 photos and successfully narrowed them down to around 800 pictures. Every one of them means something to me.

One of my client's parents traveled to Rome and Italy. We only saved about 60 of those photos, the ones containing the family on the trip and a few of the significant landmarks.

Hopefully you have some clues on which photos you can toss. The more photos you can weed out of your collection, the easier the organization will go.

Step Two – Organize by Major Category

If we organized our photos by all the separate events and moments in our lives, we would never finish. Our next step after bringing all the photos together is to organize the pictures by major category.

I recommend organizing photos chronologically for several reasons:

- Cross-referencing photos is easier when you have similar or duplicate photos to compare.

- You can refer to your Age Chart when not sure of a date and file your photo more accurately in a chronological system. (See Appendix C for a description and example.)
- When your photos are digitized, they can be labeled with the date and searched for by date.

It's okay if you want to organize photos by different categories (by person, events, etc.) I have seen successful photo organization projects when organized by person or other methods.

Here's an example list of major categories for one of our printed photo organizing projects:

- Heritage Photos (Mom's Side)
- Heritage Photos (Dad's Side)
- 1950s
- 1960s
- 1970s
- 1980s
- 1990s
- 2000s
- 2010s
- Portraits
- Career Photos
- Memorabilia
- Documents
- Photos to Give Away
- Unknown Date

Use bins and index cards to sort by major category. This is not the time to spend reminiscing over the photos. Be efficient and if you don't truly know the year, place the photos in a bin labeled "Unknown Date."

When you find envelopes and albums of photos, place those in the appropriate decade bin. You'll work with them further in the next step.

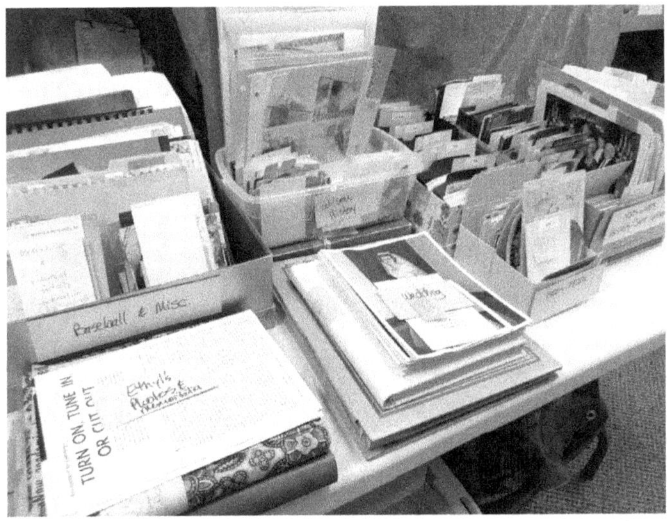

Do remove obvious duplicates, repetitive photos and bad photos as you come across them. You'll be going through the photos at least two more times, so the less you have to work with, the faster your work will go.

I can't tell you how long Step Two will take because it depends entirely on you! Will you be a "Super Sorter" and zoom through your photos, tossing the duplicates, bad photos and repetitive photos quickly and decisively? I have seen clients finish their initial sorting into categories in a weekend. Others have taken a lot longer.

There is no award for the best organizing job or fastest job! The goal is to simply finish Step Two. Do not start subdividing decades until you have sorted all of your photos by major category. Don't quit and you'll feel a great amount of success when you complete this step.

Step Three - Break Major Categories Down

Okay, we've reviewed sorting your photos into their major categories. Now we can fine tune each major category into subcategories of the organization. Again, as you go through these photos for the second time, continue to toss photos as you can. At this point, you should start remembering photos and getting a sense of what duplicates you come across.

Chronological Category Breakdown – If you sorted your photos by decades to start with, now is the time to break the decades into years where possible. For example, the major category of 1970s would be broken down as follows:

- 1970
- 1971
- 1972
- 1973
- 1974
- 1975
- 1976
- 1977
- 1978

- 1979

- 1970s – used for 1970s photos when you are not sure of the actual year in the decade

Before removing photos from envelopes, organize the envelopes by date if the envelope is dated. Then remove them and place in the corresponding year. Write the important information on the envelopes (if any) on index cards and place in your bin in front of that particular batch of photos.

Go through each major category and organize the photos further. Again, don't get sidetracked by the photos. Be efficient and keep moving!

Step Four – Fine Tune the Subcategories

Some people find that sorting by year provides a great level of organization, and they are content to stop the sorting. If you are satisfied, you could stop there.

I like to go one step further and organize by month within the years. This helps especially in the 1980s and 1990s because duplicates were so prevalent then. This part may seem tedious, but it's worth it.

Sorting by month can provide a higher level of accuracy by date and duplicate removal. It's rewarding to see groups of photos back together.

Okay – you have finally sorted and combed through your photos at least two to three times, if not more. Do you feel like your photo collection is set for the scanning process? We like to have people go through their photos one last time to weed out any final unwanted photos.

The next chapter deals with digitizing your photos with a scanner. If this Full Method of organizing your photos is not realistic, read on for the Short Cut Method.

Just Save the Important Photos – Shortcut Method

I have to say, this section really goes against all that I have taught people over the years in organizing their photos. (As is often the case, shortcuts have consequences!) But I recognize that people may need options and a quicker way to preserving their photo estate.

At Pixologie, our mission is to bring joy and peace of mind to our clients who bring us their photos and treasured memories to preserve their legacy for generations to come. If a faster method is needed, then I'm happy to offer this next way of creating your photo estate.

Please keep in mind that after your photo estate is completed with this method, you will still have a mess of photos to manage and store.

Step One – Determine Categories

What groups of photos do you want contained in your photo estate? Write down the list of categories to include. Here's some suggestions:

- Great-Grandparents
- Grandparents
- Parents
- Growing Up Years
- College, Work & Young Adulthood
- Wedding Photos
- Parenthood Photos
- Places You've Lived
- Important Friends
- Traditions
- Travel
- Up North (a common one for our clients in Wisconsin)
- 1950s, 1960s, 1970s, 1980s, etc.

You could create file folders or get an archival photo box (shoe boxes work also!) and label dividers with your categories.

Step Two – Gather Photos for Each Category

Hopefully, you remember that when we use the word "photos" we are referring to all of the different kinds of media you may have. (Refer back to page 16 to review the list.) You probably know where the majority of these photos can be found in the many places you have pictures stored. Begin going through each location and pulling out the photos you wish to preserve in your photo estate. If you intend to return photos back to albums, use a sticky note on the photo to write where it should be returned by someone in the future! (Because you most likely never will!)

Place the photos in your file folders or photo box in their respective category.

Here's a listing of all the places you might have photos:

Physical locations
- Albums
- Drawers – check them all!
- Frames
- Bins
- Closets
- Bags/baggies
- Garage/basement/attic
- Christmas cards and letters

Digital locations - (Create folders or albums of the categories and copy pictures into there – to be consolidated with the scanned photos later)
- Computers
- Camera Cards
- Smartphones (Old and Current)
- USB Drives
- External Hard Drives
- CDs/DVDs

Once you have your photos collected into their respective folders or the organizing box, you are ready for scanning which we will cover in the next chapter.

Pixologie – The study of life through your photos

(Our definition when we started Pixologie. Photo estate planning was a natural extension of organizing pictures to help families save their memories, stories and legacy.

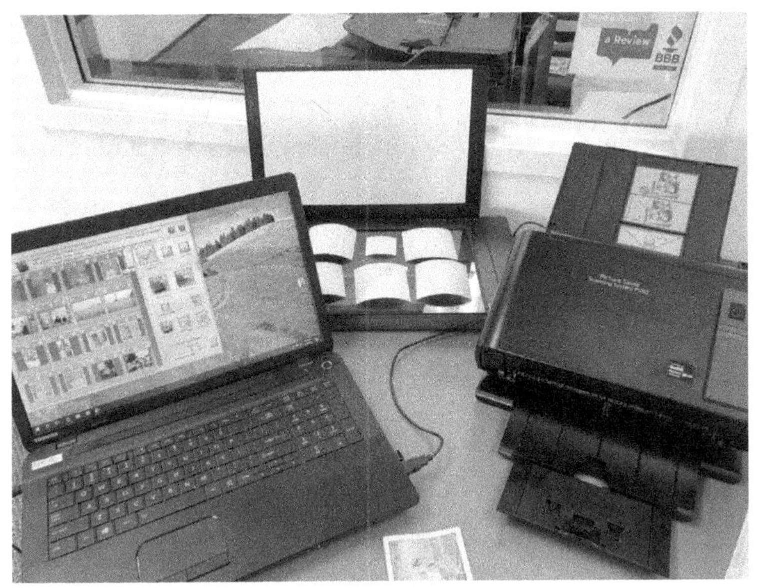

CHAPTER 3 – SCANNING YOUR PHOTOS

In order to properly preserve your photos, you'll want to scan your photos. We never recommend taking pictures or scans of your photos with your smartphone. Sometimes, for oversized or convex portraits, we use a professional camera to photograph the image properly.

Before I explain scanning options, I want to make sure you understand file formats and dpi. When you scan a photo, you want to do it the right way. If you are interested, check out Appendix D for a list of our best practices in working with client photos and other media.

File Formats

Your scanner may give you choices for saving a photo.

- JPG or JPEG – The JPG is today's standard digital photo format. Most cameras and smartphones save photos in the JPG format. Multiple edits to a JPG can result in significantly reduced quality of the original photo. We recommend scanning as JPGs for most people, however if you plan on heavy editing and multiple versions, consider scanning as a TIFF.

- TIFF –This file format is not compressed, so file sizes are very large. You can repeatedly edit a TIFF, save it and still have the same image quality achieved at first scanning. We generally see professional photographers, graphic artists and other similar professionals using this file format. File sizes are so large (30 to 100 MB), that working with them can be very slow.

- PDF – A PDF is a document, not an image. We never scan photos as PDFs for obvious reasons. We do scan some of the memorabilia and documents in a photo collection as PDFs if it makes sense. (Narratives, documents with multiple pages, etc.)

There are a few other formats of photos you may come across in your digital photo collection.

- PNG – This file format allows easy digital sharing with small file sizes. You create a PNG when you take a screenshot of something on your computer, tablet or smartphone.

- HEIF – Apple's newest photo format on iPhones.

- Camera Raw Formats – extensions vary based on what camera you are using. Generally, used by professional photographers

DPI – What Resolution to Use?

Most scanners allow you to change the scanning resolution setting or the DPI setting. DPI stands for dots per inch and the higher the DPI, the more detail is caught as you scan the image.

Scanning DPI generally can range from 72 DPI up to 1200 DPI. As you can imagine, the higher the DPI, the larger the digital file size. For photo scanning, we recommend scanning at 600 DPI. This is the accepted archival standard.

Okay, now that we have covered file formats and resolution, let's talk about some of the scanning options available.

Scanning Options

Depending upon the number of photos you have to scan, you'll want to think about which option may be right for you. Also, are many of your photos fragile or stuck to album pages? You may need more than one type of scanner.

Your Printer/Scanner - Yes, you can scan photos with your printer/scanner in a pinch if you need. Using your printer to scan a large number of photos takes a very long time and may not offer high enough resolution for a quality scan. Be aware, an image that looks good on the computer may not have enough DPI to print it. Typically, your printer scanner comes with software that allows you to save your scans in a folder on your computer.

Here's a screenshot of the software that is on my Mac to scan photos and documents. When I opened it, the resolution was set to 75 dpi and format was set to JPEG. You can also see the words "Scan To" which allows you to locate exactly where on your computer to save the scans. I don't have the option of naming the images. However, I can place several pictures on the scanner and Auto Selection will detect and save separate items.

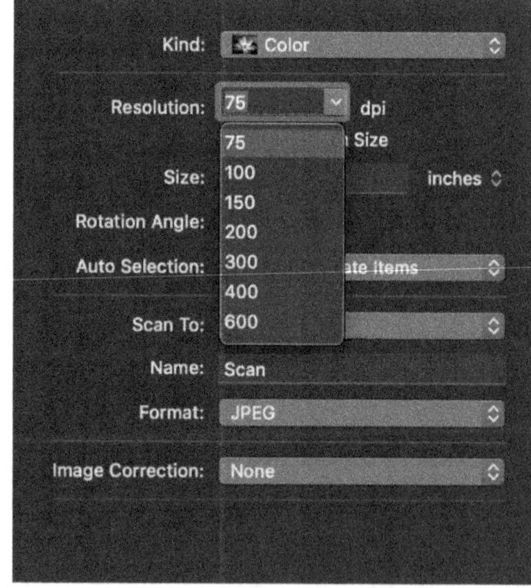

The Kodak Alaris Picture Saver Scanning System – We love this scanning system because it combines high speed scanning along with flatbed scanning as we need it.

You can digitize up to 1,000 photos an hour with the high-speed scanner. There is also an easy option to scan the backsides of the photos automatically. Then, when you have a fragile photo, you can switch the scanning to the flatbed. You can work back and forth as needed.

Unfortunately, Kodak Alaris has discontinued making the Picture Saver Scanning System. Nationwide, people can rent the scanners through E-Z Photo Scan with their Rent2Scan program. You can find their contact information in the Resources at the end of this book.

The Epson FastFoto FF-680W Wireless High-speed Photo and Document Scanning System – Priced around $500-600, this consumer grade scanner has been earning high reviews all the way around.

While not as heavy duty of a machine as the Kodak Alaris scanners, the Epson can scan one photo a second at 300 DPI. At 600 DPI, it still scans your photos fast. For fragile photos and documents, Epson offers carrier sheets to send the photos through the scanner.

We have clients who have purchased this scanner and are very happy with its performance.

Flip-Pal Mobile Scanner – Some people enjoy having a simple, portable scanner to digitize photos. The Flip-Pal has been a favorite tool of ours for many years. It allows you to scan photos wherever you are because it is battery powered. (Perfect for family reunions.) While it's flatbed only fits 4 x 6 photos, the Flip-Pal comes with software to stitch scanned sections of a larger photograph together.

The Flip-Pal has a small screen so you can see your photo as it is scanned. Also, the cover can be removed, and the scanner turned upside down to scan photos stuck on album pages.

You will need to crop the photos at a later point. But you'll find this easy as you simply transfer the photos on the Flip-Pal's SD card to your computer. Then edit with your program of choice. The Flip-Pal can be purchased for around $180 through Pixologie or Flip-Pal directly.

Many other flatbed photo scanner options – Epson and other companies make a variety of flatbed scanners which are considerably less expensive than the high-speed scanner options listed. Each has its own advantages and disadvantages.

Naming Your Scanned Photos

Keep in mind the following definitions when naming your scanned photos:

- Folders – hold the scanned photos
- Files – are the photos, documents, etc.

When working with photos typically, our standard for naming digital folders is:

YYYY-MM-DD Description

You complete the name with as much detail as reasonable. This is not the place for a 20-word description! Here are some variations of its use:

- 1900s-1930s Photos
- 1976 Family Photos
- 2013-12-25 Christmas Photos

By naming folders this way, the folders organize chronologically automatically. Inside, your scanned or digital photos can be named the same if your scanner allows you to choose how files are named.

Starting Scanning

When you start scanning batches of photos, please be sure to check your output folders to ensure your files are being scanned and named as you expected.

As you go about scanning photos, remember to switch to new folders and naming when you start the next family batch of photos. When you are done scanning, you can take the next steps with the printed photos including:

- Throwing the photos away or recycling the ones which are safe to do so
- Returning them to where they came from
- Storing in an archival photo box - You may wish to purchase photo and document safe storage for your collection either

before or after you have completed your organization. We sell a variety of archival boxes.

Archival Quality Storage Boxes

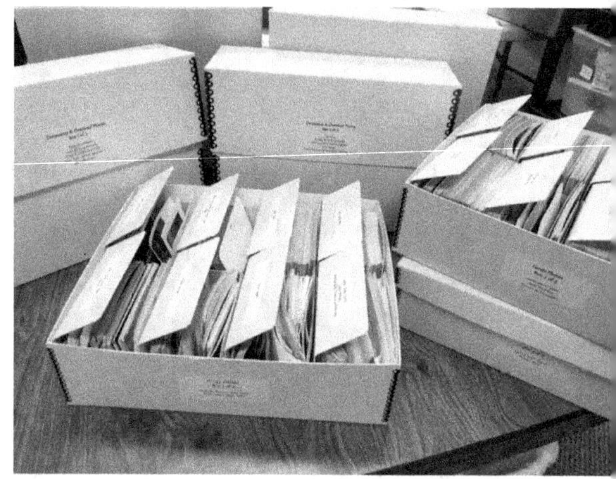

Look for your archiving products to be PVC, lignin and acid free. If you are storing other fragile items with non-paper characteristics (leather, etc.), you should also explore whether products should be buffered. Buffered boxes and paper contain properties to help counteract acids that may form in the material being preserved.

Newspaper clippings and other non-photo materials should be preserved separately from photos. These materials can contain acid and can cause damage to your photos in the long-term.

Okay, this stage of your photo estate is complete, now we must figure out how your digital files will preserve the stories within the pictures. Proper documentation is needed.

CHAPTER 4 – BRINGING THE FILES TOGETHER

Once you have your photos scanned, you'll need to bring those files together with the digital photos you've identified to be included in your photo estate. You can do this with file folders in Windows and on a Mac computer. Or, you may want to use a photo organizing program.

There are many software programs and websites available for you to preserve your photos. I have worked with clients attempting to teach them to use their programs. However, I have found that the vast majority don't use the programs often enough to remember basic functions. And, software programs and apps are now frequently updated, so the program doesn't even look the same when people return to use it. Lastly, photo software and app companies come and go frequently, and one cannot rely on the software being around for the long term. (Anyone ever use Picasa, Carousel or Aperture?)

For these reasons, I'll show examples using a simple file folder system on a PC computer using File Explorer and on a Mac computer using Finder.

Windows Digital Folders Using Windows Explorer

s PC › Pictures › Family Photo Estate ›

Name	Date	Type	Size	Tags
1930s and Earlier	1/15/2020 5:59 AM	File folder		
1940s	1/15/2020 6:00 AM	File folder		
1950s	1/15/2020 6:00 AM	File folder		
1960s	1/15/2020 6:01 AM	File folder		
1970s	1/15/2020 6:01 AM	File folder		
1980s	1/15/2020 6:01 AM	File folder		
1990s	1/15/2020 6:01 AM	File folder		
2000s	1/15/2020 6:02 AM	File folder		
2010s	1/15/2020 6:02 AM	File folder		
Career	1/15/2020 6:02 AM	File folder		
Christmas Cards	1/15/2020 6:02 AM	File folder		
Grandpa Hartmann - Military Service	1/15/2020 6:02 AM	File folder		
Grandparents - Hartmann	1/15/2020 6:03 AM	File folder		
Grandparents - Kordus	1/15/2020 6:03 AM	File folder		
Grandparents - Luke	1/15/2020 6:03 AM	File folder		
Grandparents - Ostroski	1/15/2020 6:03 AM	File folder		
Portraits	1/15/2020 6:03 AM	File folder		
Travel	1/15/2020 6:04 AM	File folder		

Mac Digital Folders Using Finder

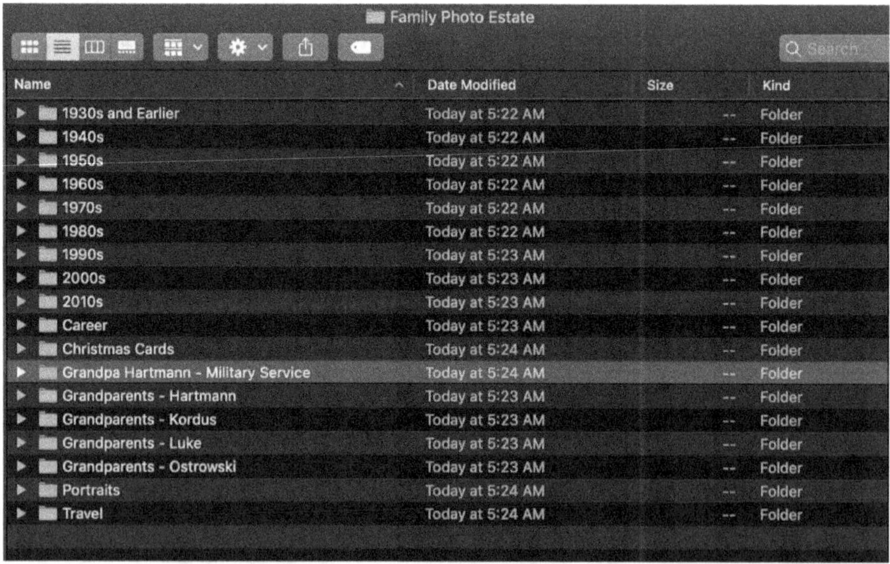

Family Photo Estate

Name	Date Modified	Size	Kind
1930s and Earlier	Today at 5:22 AM	--	Folder
1940s	Today at 5:22 AM	--	Folder
1950s	Today at 5:22 AM	--	Folder
1960s	Today at 5:22 AM	--	Folder
1970s	Today at 5:22 AM	--	Folder
1980s	Today at 5:22 AM	--	Folder
1990s	Today at 5:23 AM	--	Folder
2000s	Today at 5:23 AM	--	Folder
2010s	Today at 5:23 AM	--	Folder
Career	Today at 5:23 AM	--	Folder
Christmas Cards	Today at 5:24 AM	--	Folder
Grandpa Hartmann - Military Service	Today at 5:24 AM	--	Folder
Grandparents - Hartmann	Today at 5:23 AM	--	Folder
Grandparents - Kordus	Today at 5:23 AM	--	Folder
Grandparents - Luke	Today at 5:23 AM	--	Folder
Grandparents - Ostrowski	Today at 5:23 AM	--	Folder
Portraits	Today at 5:24 AM	--	Folder
Travel	Today at 5:24 AM	--	Folder

Create subfolders for the subcategories you've designated. (For example, 1970s would contain individual folders for 1970 through 1979, if desired.)

If you wish to use other programs, here's some that we have recommended:

- Forever® Historian
- Mylio
- Adobe Bridge (great for batch cropping and renaming – high learning curve, but easier to use than Adobe Lightroom)
- Photos for Mac – comes installed

Try out a few options if you are looking for photo organizing software. Be sure you enjoy using the software. This will keep you motivated to return and work on your photo estate project, and family photo management in general.

Information about the photo on next page: Front row, left to right: Louisa Glade, Emma Veidt, Mary Bullerdick, Minna Griebel, Hannah Faberdinger. Back row, left to right: John Efferding, Louis Charles Efferding, William Henry Efferding, Lena Harms, Alice Yeager. Thankfully, someone took the time decades ago to write who was who in this important photo.

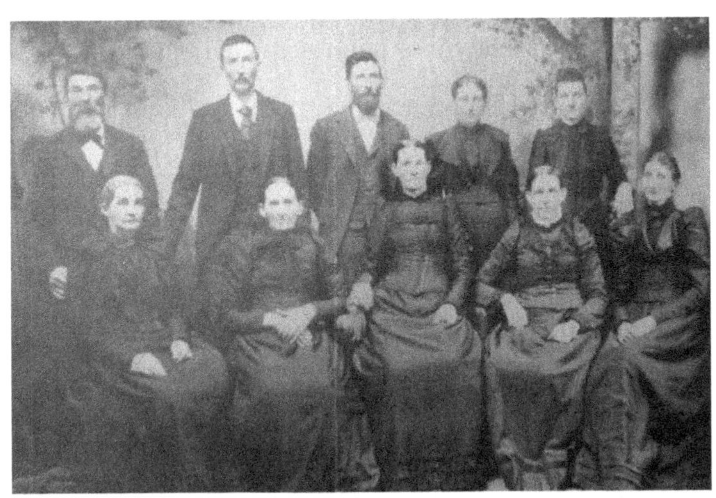

CHAPTER 5 – DOCUMENTATION

Remember that part of our definition of a photo estate, *"learn about the lives documented?"* You are probably still wondering how this information can be added to your digital photos.

There are three main ways we add documentation to people's photos. They are:

1. Scanning the backsides of the photos.
2. Captions and narratives added into a book or printed document with your photos.
3. Metadata (digital information) added to a photo

Scanning the backsides of the photo

We often scan both front and backsides of photos. The handwritten notes can be quite helpful for dating and for storytelling. Here's an example of some scanned photos with information on the back.

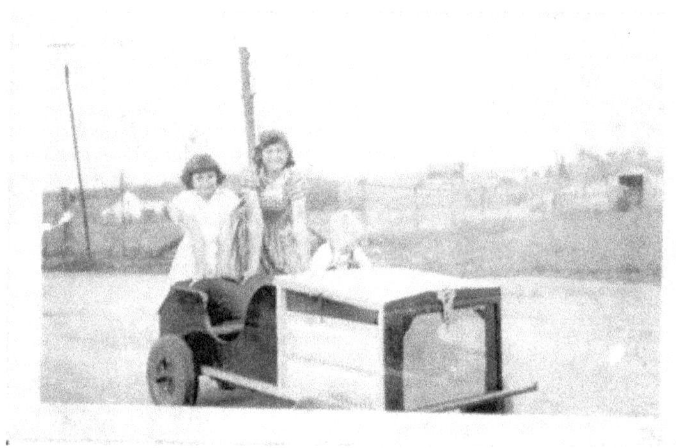

1949
Dorothy · age 12
Carol · age 8 David · age 2
Florence & Leon's house to the left. Fur
shed in mink yard at right, built by Pa
and us kids

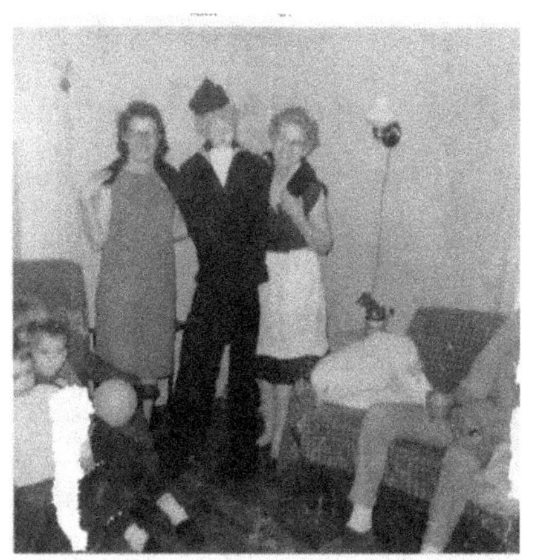

However, it's hard to know that both the front and the backside of the digital photos will remain together in their digital folder or album. And, not every photo has written information on the back. So, this isn't a really good long-term solution for adding documentation to your photo collection.

Captions and narratives in a book or document

Would you like to have your photo estate printed? A treasure that you can physically hold in your hand? Books can include photo books, pictorial histories, memoirs. Other documents can be created with an index of the photos and a caption or description added. These can be spiral bound and shared with family also.

You can easily order additional copies of the books for each family member. And, you can preserve a digital version of the book for people to access in the future and order reprints.

Photo Book – Created through an online website such as Shutterfly, Snapfish, Blurb or FOREVER® among many other options. You can use the online templates to create a photo book that brings your heritage and legacy to life. Add names, places and stories to go with the photos. If you are interested in this kind of book, consider reading *"The Pixologist's Guide to Creating a Meaningful Photo Book"* available on Amazon.

Pictorial History & Memoirs – These books look more like a textbook and can have hundreds of pages. I've seen clients use Microsoft Publisher to create these books and order through websites like Blurb. These books have significantly more narrative and may also contain copies of genealogy papers and much more. Others have hired a personal historian to complete their book.

Document Index of Photos with Descriptions – You could create a document with all of your photos and type a description for each picture. Then, you can save the file as a PDF that can be shared with the rest of the family.

Printed books give you and your family a tangible treasure to enjoy. Preserve the digital format as a PDF to ensure the book is accessible for future generations.

With all of these book and document options, however, there is a significant downside. The information is not connected to the digital photo itself. If those books or documents disappear, a lot of knowledge will be lost about who's who and what's important in the preserved photos.

However, on the flip side, we could have a major worldwide disaster wiping out all of our technology. If ever technology were to disappear, these books and your archival photo boxes may be the only connection our future families have to us. It would be just like it is today when we look back at our own ancestors' old heirloom photos, fragile, dusty documents in old script and crumbling black scrapbooks.

Let's hope that doesn't happen. Next we'll talk about adding metadata to your digital photos.

Metadata added to a photo

First, you may already know that every digital picture has information embedded in its file. This information is called metadata and includes:

- File name
- Date photo was taken (or created in the event it was scanned)
- Type of camera/scanner used
- Film size
- Dimensions
- Location
- And much more

The metadata essentially has fields that are filled in based on what is known about the photo. There are some fields that can be edited such as:

- Tags/Keywords
- Comments/Description
- Rating
- Date taken
- Copyright

The two fields I focus on are:

- **Tags or Keywords** – Simple terms or names that you can add to photos. You can then search by tag and view all the photos with that person or subject. (i.e. Dogs, Up North, Grandma Kordus)
- **Comments/Description** – Here, you can add commentary about the photo. Who's in it, what's going on, where it was taken and more. (i.e. This is Helen Kordus on a girl's road trip to Nebraska back in the 1930s.)

In my years as a professional photo organizer, I have found very few people know how to add metadata to a photo. It does take some computer software know-how and it takes time to do it. You also need to use a computer to add metadata to a photo. (For our favorite SIMPLE solution to adding metadata on any device, skip the rest of this chapter and read Chapter 7.)

If you are looking for software to add metadata, I have worked with clients to use FOREVER® Historian, Mylio, Adobe Bridge and Adobe Lightroom. These all require some learning and routine use to keep familiar with their features.

For the purposes of this book, I will just focus on one way to add metadata for Windows users and one option for Mac as well as an option that works with both computer systems.

Adding Metadata for Windows Users

Windows computers offer a straightforward way to access your photos metadata and edit the information. Windows uses the terms "Tags" and "Comments." Here's the steps to adding metadata with Windows 10:

1. Open Windows File Explorer to the desired folder
2. Right-click on the photo/s for which you wish to add tags or descriptions
3. Select properties. The following should appear, be sure to click the "Details" tab.
4. Add your tags and comments and then click okay.

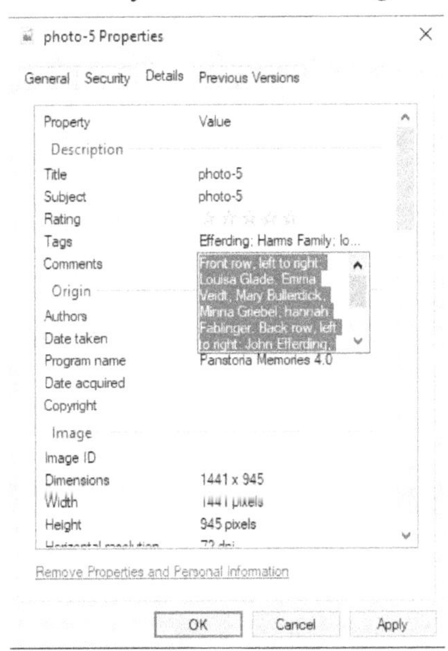

Adding Metadata for Mac Users

Normally, Mac users have an advantage when working with photos. However, in this case, if you wish to add metadata to your photos, you will need a program that has metadata editing capability.

You can use Photos, the photo organization software installed on your Mac to add metadata. This very much complicates the folder structure that I described earlier. Once the metadata is added, you will then either leave the photos in that program or export them back to a new set of folders. For those people who like using Photos, that is fine. But this is not a long-term solution to ensuring your photo estate can be passed on to future generations.

Using Photos to Add Metadata

- Imported the pictures into your Photos program
- While holding your control key down, click on a photo
- Select "Get Info"
- Add Description and Keyword to the photos metadata. (In the screenshot, you can see the other information available.

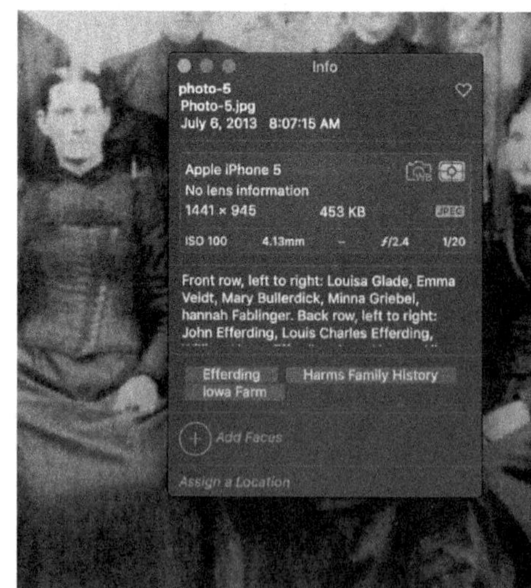

Both Windows and Mac users can use Adobe Bridge or Adobe Lightroom to add metadata. With these programs, you can add the information to the original file in its folder. (This will avoid the importing and exporting of the photo out of a program like Photos.) Bridge is available as a free download or packaged with Adobe Creative Suite's Photography Plan for $9.99 per month if you wish to edit photos.

Using Adobe Bridge to add metadata

1. Start Adobe Bridge and go to the folder where your photos are located.

2. (PC) Right click on the photo and select "File Info." (MAC) Holding the Control key down, click on the photo and select "File Info"

3. Add your information and click okay.

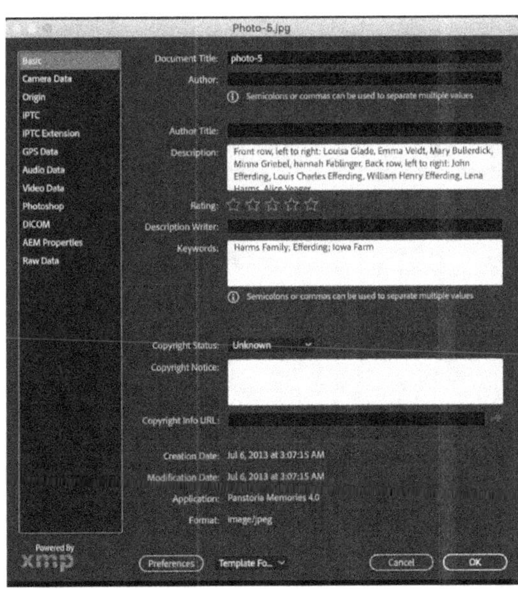

With Windows Explorer, Mac Photos and Adobe Bridge, you can select a group of photos and add the information as well.

Now you probably know a lot more about metadata and how to add it, which is an important step. But it sure isn't easy or enjoyable to look at the photos and read about who is in the pictures. It's really unbelievable in this day and age that the metadata can be so difficult to access.

I'll show you in Chapter 7 how this information can be added easily and can be viewed side by side with the photo.

CHAPTER 6 – KEEP YOUR PHOTO ESTATE SAFE

By now, hopefully, you've seen a path to creating your photo estate and maybe, you've even started on the journey and are close to completion.

Next, it's important to ensure your photo estate is safe and backed up. Most people still store their photo collections on their computers. This presents a risk as computer hard drives will fail and humans can make errors. We recommend that your photo estate be backed up in two other locations. You can find many options for backing up your photos including physical hard drive back-ups as well as cloud-based back-ups. We recommend you have one back-up in the house and one outside of the house, preferably outside your city.

External Hard Dive Back-Up Options

Both PC and Mac computers come with software to connect to an external hard drive. You can set the back-up to occur as often as you like. You can also simply copy your photo estate to the external hard drive. Remember to update the back-up if you add photos to your photo estate collection on your computer. Unless you schedule this back-up/update on your calendar, it is unlikely that you will keep it up to date.

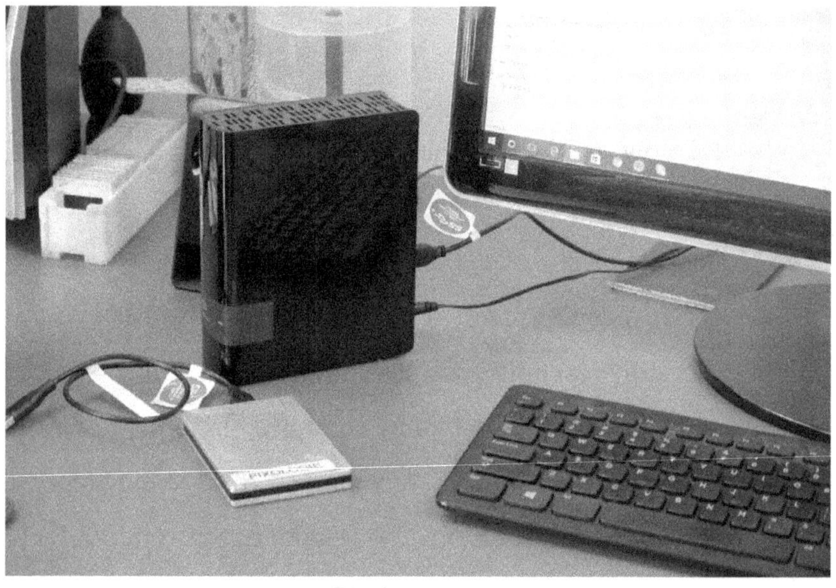

Above, a photo of two types of external hard drives, one small portable and one large desktop drive. Either one will work for your in-home back-up.

For your second copy stored outside the house, you could use another external hard drive. You might put it in a safe deposit box or at a family member's home.

Cloud Based Back-Up Options

For your photo estate, I don't believe using a computer back-up service like Carbonite or Backblaze is good enough. But it is better than no outside backup at all. These services back up all your computer's files to their online services.

In the event of a computer crash, the company will send your files back for you to restore to your computer. You could be without your files for a good period of time. We've had reports of clients who were unable to recover their photo collections as well, but this could be due to user error.

These computer back-up services do not allow for easy viewing and enjoyment of your photo collection.

The internet offers "free" cloud storage for photos including sites like Google. Paid cloud storages include Amazon, Dropbox among many others. For Mac users, Apple offers iCloud, but many consumers don't understand how it works.

We caution our clients about most website photo storage for reasons including:

- Some "free" sites pay for storing your photos by selling your information or even access to your photos. If you use one of these sites, be sure to review the agreement and make sure you are not signing away the rights to your personal photos. And be aware, your personal information may be used for marketing research and other purposes. Free also means no obligation to you. Terms can change anytime.

- With the fast mergers, changes and closures that occur in technology companies, the website may not be around in a few years. We have had clients lose access to their photos because the company closed or merged with another company and service ended for online photo storage.
- The photo storage site may not keep the highest resolution of your photo.
- For paid storage sites, storage only lasts as long as you pay. One client lost years of historical photos when she did not realize her credit card had expired.
- Photos may be difficult to download and may not retain the metadata of the photo – so important to telling your story!
- After you are gone, there is no guarantee your family will have access to the photos you have preserved.

For short term reasons, some of these websites may be beneficial to having a second back-up of your photo collection. However, you might be interested to learn of a more permanent cloud solution.

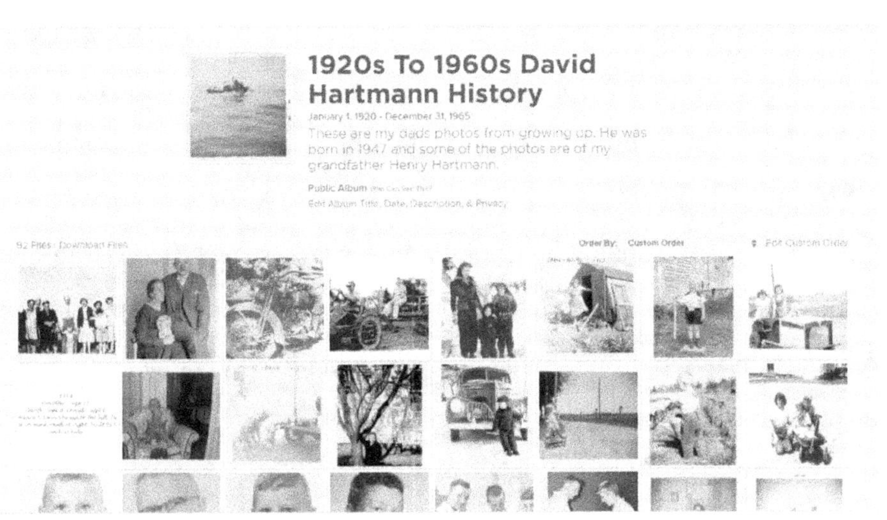

CHAPTER 7 – FOREVER®

Imagine you spent a good amount of time and money working with me, a photo organizing expert and photo estate planner. I've taught you how to use your computer and your photo organizing program. After our time is finished, how long will you maintain your digital photo organization? Time and life will intervene, and you probably won't get back to your pictures too often.

I have found that my time is best spent with clients teaching them to use a solution for their photos that is simple. No more providing training on complicated photo organizing programs.

FOREVER® permanent cloud storage offers all that our clients need to preserve their photo estates. Over the past six years, we have watched a company named Forever, Inc. develop permanent cloud photo storage. We participated in its early beta testing, provide ongoing feedback for improvements, and currently have over 500 clients storing photos in FOREVER®.

I have personally lost photos and print projects stored online with companies that have gone out of business. Sometimes, these companies provide no warning and consumers lose precious memories and hard work. We are very careful on what we recommend to our clients for this reason.

Forever, Inc. appears much different in scope. Glen Meakem, the founder, wanted a place where his family could store all of their family photos, video and documents once and for all. He envisioned this collection being passed on to future generations. A portion of the storage purchase price goes into a fund that allows the company to guarantee your content will be preserved for your lifetime plus 100 years. From Forever, Inc.'s website:

> *FOREVER® isn't like other photo storage services. We're focused on providing you with a permanent digital home that will last for generations. It's like insurance for your photos.*™

You can purchase 10GB of storage for a one-time fee of $199 which can hold 2,500 to 5,000 photos. A portion of that purchase goes into the "FOREVER®" Guarantee Fund which promises to migrate your photos to the newest technology for the next 100 years. Glen Meakem envisions Forever as an institution lasting hundreds of years and more, keeping family legacies safe.

Below are the albums in one of our client's accounts. She has over 9,000 in her photo estate and loves looking at the photos on her computer, phone and iPad.

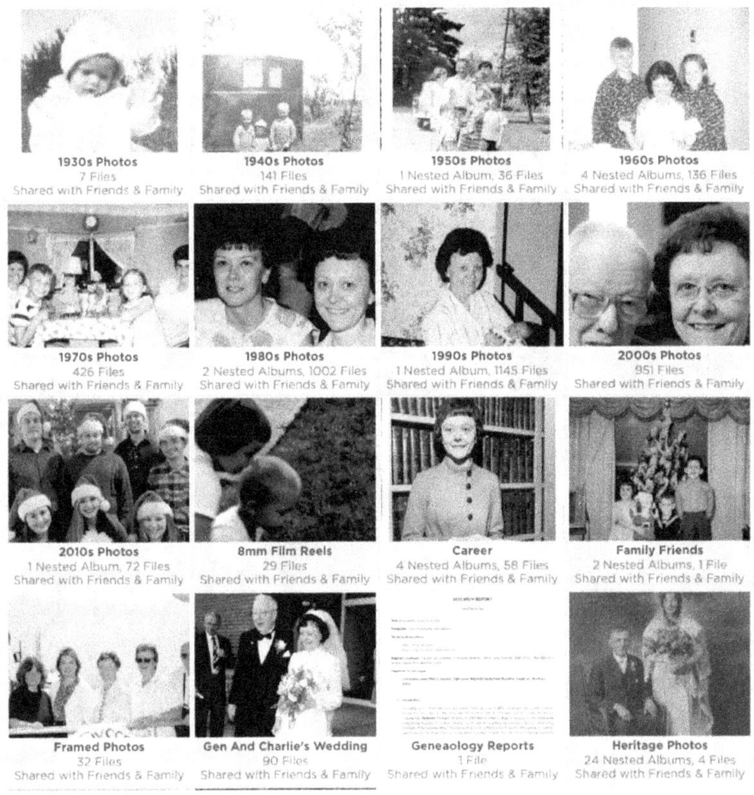

Even with storing photos in FOREVER®, I still recommend keeping a digital back-up in your home. Your FOREVER® account is accessed through internet connection. If you are without internet and/or electricity, you will not have access to your Forever account.

Better than a digital back-up, create a printed photo book with the highlights of your family history. Then, you can have all your photos safe in a permanent cloud storage site and a physical book containing the highlights of your photo estate.

For a complimentary trial account, please visit: www.forever.com/ambassador/pixologie. You'll receive 2 GB of storage, enough for 200-500 photos and a $10 coupon.

Pixologie is a FOREVER® Ambassador and does receive commissions from client purchases.

CHAPTER 8 – BEFORE & AFTER PICTURES

Wonder how other people got through their photo estate projects? We've seen many wonderful photo collections come together into a rich history of memories, images, stories and legacy. Enjoy looking at what other people started with and how their projects ended!

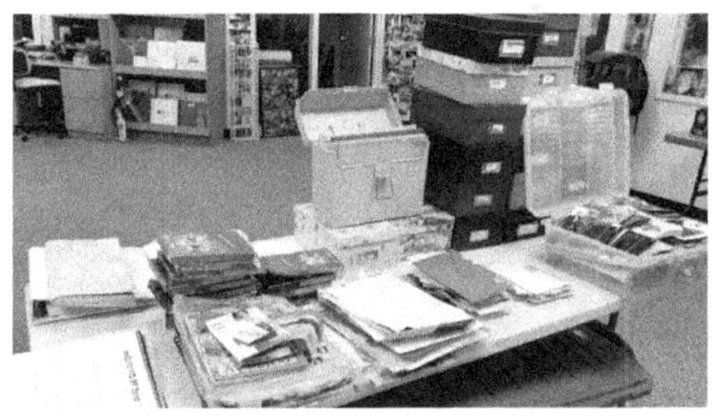

BEFORE

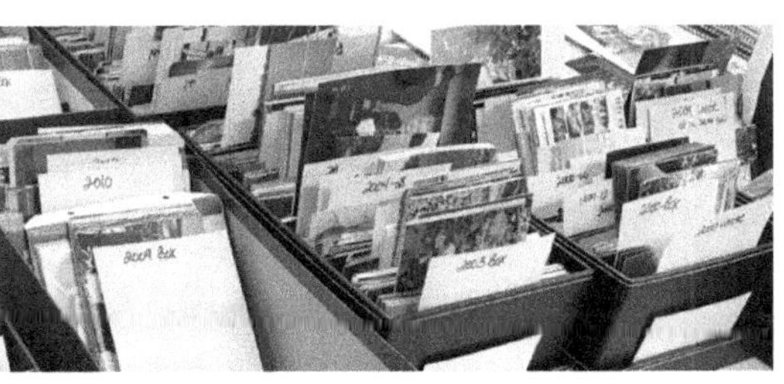

AFTER

Organized, ready for scanning

Kelly's Project

Kelly inherited photos from her grandmother and also had her mother's. You can read her moving story on our website under "Client Stories."

BEFORE

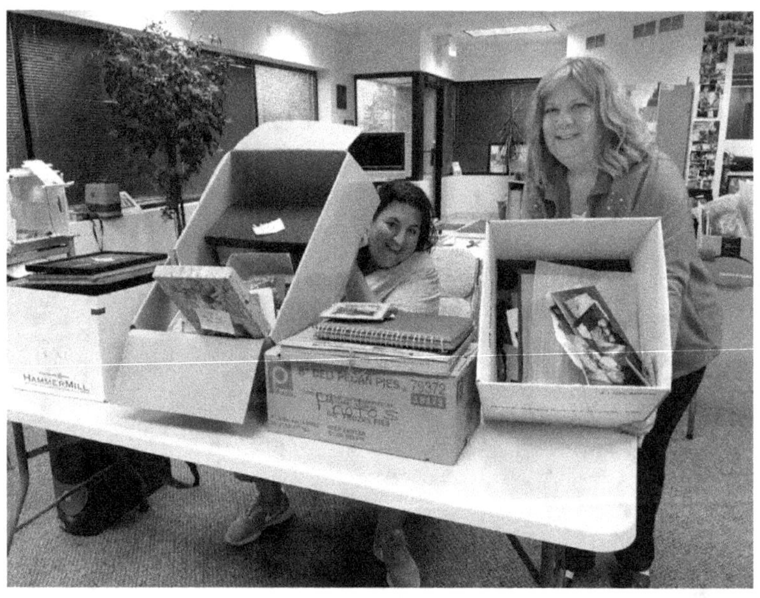

AFTER

Kelly's finished photo estate included an archival box and her family's photos in a FOREVER® account.

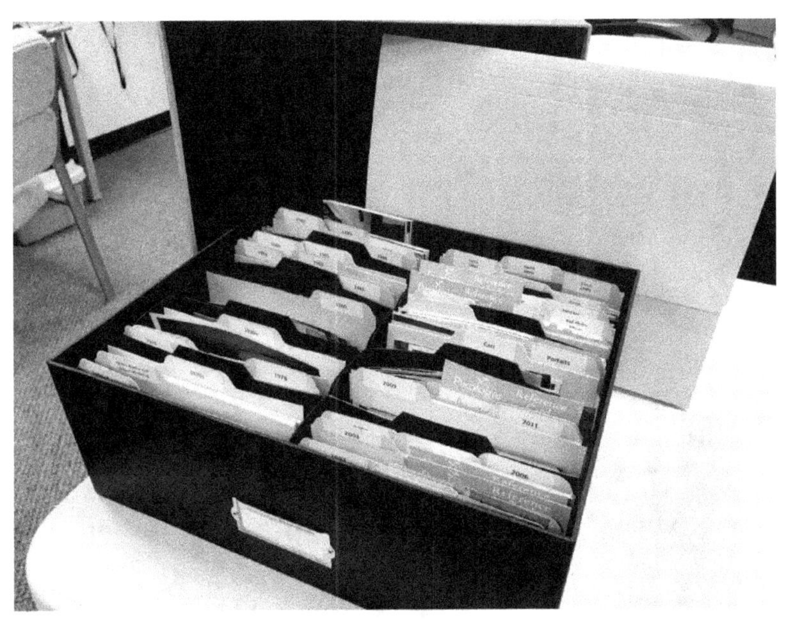

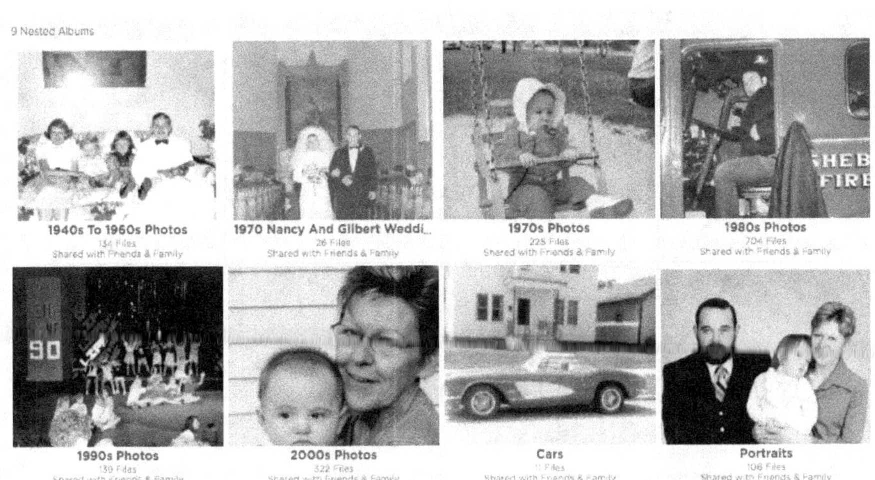

Gen's Project

Gen's photo collection included extremely old photos from her aunts and grandparents. Her photo estate (including all of the old farm documents, immigration papers and more) came to over 9,000 scanned images. Her photo estate is also online.

You've seen her completed photo estate on pages 48 and 67. Her estate also included over 1500 slides and 15 reels of film.

BEFORE

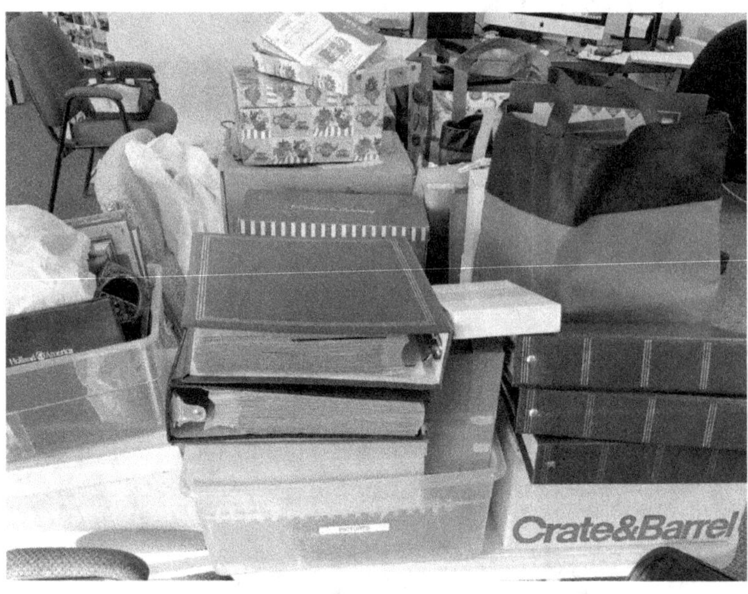

AFTER

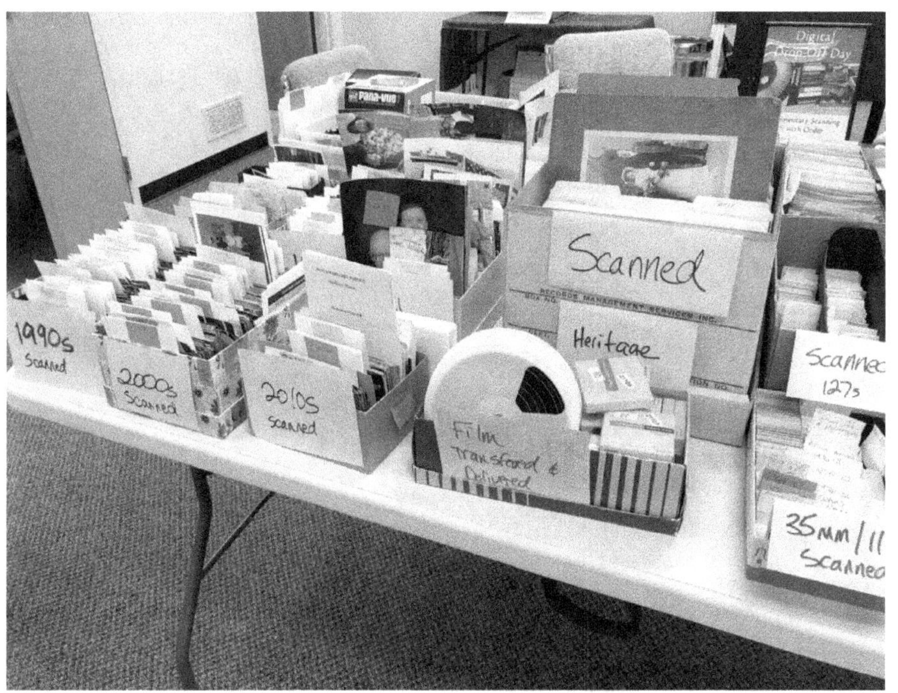

When we were finished with Gen's project, she told she felt as though her life was restored.

Boxes of Photo Envelopes

Here's an example of how one client's boxes of photo envelopes were broken down into years. Batches of photos were stacked, and many duplicates removed.

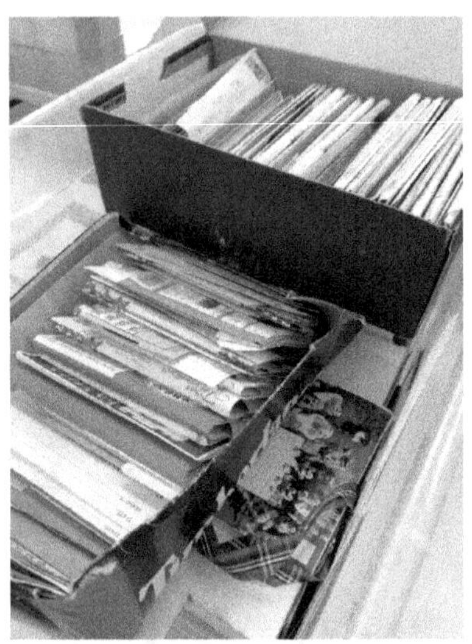

BEFORE & AFTER

There were four large bins of photo envelopes just like these.

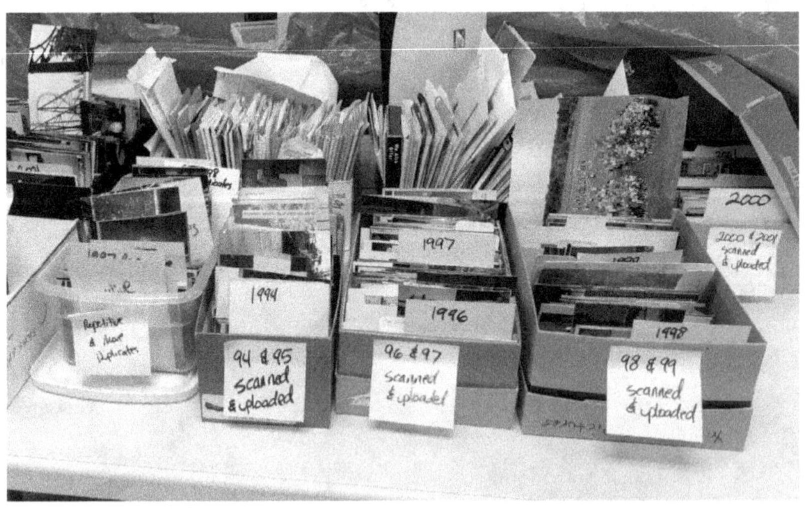

CHAPTER 9 – WHEN YOU NEED HELP

Depending up on the size of your photo collection, you may decide it's too much to handle on your own. Consider hiring a photo estate planner or professional photo organizer. Hourly rates vary from $75 to $125 per hour. You can search online to find a professional photo organizer near you. Be sure to ask for references and read reviews.

We've worked with long-distance clients at Pixologie and are happy to assist you with your project.

Pixologie Contact Information

Please visit our website for the latest news, posts and information on our studio and services.

Website: www.pixologieinc.com

Address: 9803 S. 13th Street, Oak Creek, WI 53154

Phone number: 414-731-1881

Email: contact@pixologieinc.com

Follow us on Facebook, Twitter, Instagram, LinkedIn and YouTube!

Pixologie's Website

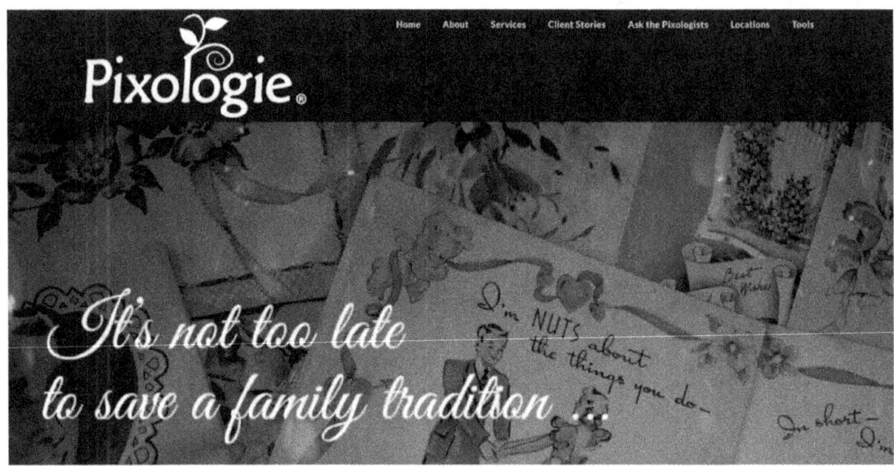

Experts in Photo Estate Planning™, Photo Organizing and Memory Preservation

After six years and over one million photos saved, our clients have started calling us their "Pixologists." Whether you want to figure out how to organize photos yourself or you want to hire us to do it, we've got answers for you.

Don't know where to start? Click here for blog posts, tools and even schedule a complimentary 15 minute phone consultation.

Our Latest News

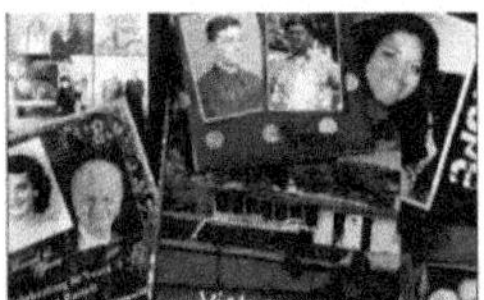

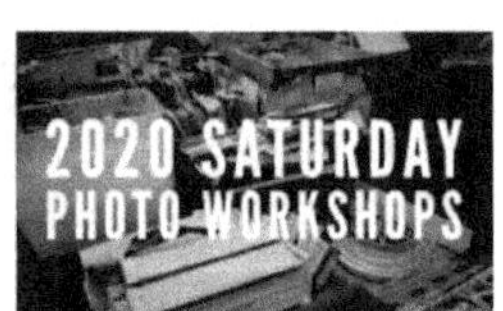

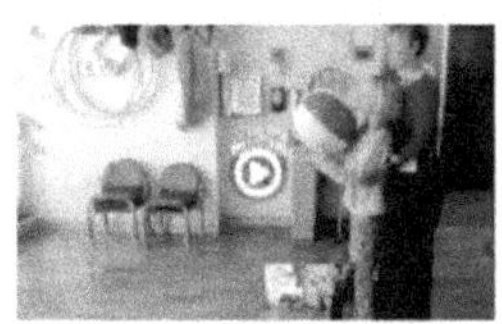

What is the Best Way to Make a Photo Book?

Today, it is easier than ever to make a photo book. We've been asked, "What ...

Read More

2020 Photo Workshops

Pixologie's Photo Workshops promise 12 hours of dedicated time for your photo projects. Come and ...

Read More

Add a Video to a Photo Book

Wouldn't it be great to open a photo book and be able to watch a ...

Read More

IN CONCLUSION

Thank you so much for learning about what it takes to create a photo estate, a worthy legacy on its own. I hope you are well on your journey to preserving your family's history.

If you are looking for more than a quick guide, I highly encourage you to purchase "The Pixologist's Guide to Organizing Your Family Photos" which provides much more detail, client examples and color photos.

I wish you all the best as you bring your photo estate together. I'd love to hear from you about your progress as well as any feedback you may have. Feel free to contact me in several ways:

- LinkedIn: linkedin.com/in/molliebartelt
- Facebook: facebook.com/pixologie
- Twitter: twitter.com/pixologie
- Email: mollieb@pixologieinc.com

Cheers and blessings to you!
Mollie

***People have no idea how time flies
and the opportunity to save
the stories from photos is lost forever.***

***Clients have told us, "I can sleep better
at night knowing this is done!***

APPENDIX A – 20 QUESTIONS

Back in 2001, Dr. Fivush and Dr. Marshall Duke, of Emory University created a list of twenty questions. These simple questions help parents talk about family history topics with their children. Can you answer these questions?

Twenty Questions

- Do you know how your parents met?
- Do you know where your mother grew up?
- Do you know where your father grew up?
- Do you know where some of your grandparents grew up?
- Do you know where some of your grandparents met?
- Do you know where your parents were married?
- Do you know what went on when you were being born?
- Do you know the source of your name?
- Do you know some things about what happened when your brothers or sisters were being born?
- Do you know which person in your family you look most like?
- Do you know which person in the family you act most like?

- Do you know some of the illnesses and injuries that your parents experienced when they were younger?
- Do you know some of the lessons that your parents learned from good or bad experiences?
- Do you know some things that happened to your mom or dad when they were in school?
- Do you know the national background of your family (such as English, German, Russian, etc.)?
- Do you know some of the jobs that your parents had when they were young?
- Do you know some awards that your parents received when they were young?
- Do you know the names of the schools that your mom went to?
- Do you know the names of the schools that your dad went to?
- Do you know about a relative whose face "froze" in a grumpy position because he or she did not smile enough?

Be sure to talk about these questions at family gatherings. Then, be sure to add the answers to your photo estate by adding the stories to a photo book, by videotaping responses, or even audio recording family responses.

APPENDIX B — AGE CHART

Do you want to more easily date photos? The Age Chart provides ESSENTIAL clues to dating pictures, especially for those people who have children.

If you are organizing a large collection of photos with multiple families, a more expansive timeline may be required. Just apply the same principles of known dates and events (weddings, funerals, immigration dates, etc.)

You'll see on the next page an age chart for my family. For other clients, we've had as many as eight columns for one large family. Clients have expanded the concept to go back several generations as well.

You can download a customizable Age Chart from our website at: www.pixologieinc.com/tools.

The Pixologist's Guide to Organizing Photos –

Age Chart Example

Here's an example of a family with two children. Change the names and dates for your photo organization project. The next page is a simplified form with columns for four children.

Year	Child #1 – Mollie		Child #2 - Rosie	
	Age	Grade	Age	Grade
1972	Born 9/3/1972			
1973	1			
1974	2		Born 7/1/1974	
1975	3		1	
1976	4		2	
1977	5	Preschool	3	
1978	6	Preschool/1st	4	
1979	7	First/Second	5	Preschool
1980	8	Second/Third	6	Preschool/1st
1981	9	Third/Fourth	7	First/Second
1982	10	Fourth/Fifth	8	Second/Third
1983	11	Fifth/Sixth	9	Third/Fourth
1984	12	Sixth/Seventh	10	Fourth/Fifth
1985	13	Seventh/Eighth	11	Fifth/Sixth
1986	14	Eighth/Freshman	12	Sixth/Seventh
1987	15	Freshman/Sophomore	13	Seventh/Eighth
1988	16	Sophomore/Junior	14	Eighth/Freshman
1989	17	Junior/Senior	15	Freshman/Sophomore
1990	18	Senior – Graduated HS	16	Sophomore/Junior
1991	19		17	Junior/Senior
1992	20		18	Senior – Graduated HS
Other Milestones	1994 – Graduated College 1996 - Wedding		1998 - Wedding	

APPENDIX C – BEST PRACTICES

When we launched Pixologie in 2013, we had a clear vision of bringing photo organization into a recognized and valued service business where consumers can get their stories told and preserved for future generations.

There are too many options for consumers, too many ways to save a photo and too little time to figure it out. Pixologie is changing this by offering clear industry standards for the photo organization and management field and to our licensees who are operating their own independent businesses.

Over the past seven years, we dived deep into developing photo organization standards, digital file format best practices and levels of service.

Preservation Level – Generally for consumers, family photo collections

- Printed photos are sorted, stored in photo safe, archival quality boxes
- Scanned photos are 300 or 600 dpi, saved as superior, quality JPGs.

- Digital photos are saved as JPGs

- Slides and negatives are scanned at 2000 dpi and saved as JPGs

- Videos and film are transferred to a digital file – MP4

- Back-up includes two digital copies, one onsite (off the main computer) and one offsite

Archival Level – For professional photographers, business and historical photo collections

- Printed photos, slides, negatives are sorted, stored in photo safe, archival quality boxes

- Scanned photos are 600 dpi, saved as TIFs, once edits are completed, can be saved as JPGs

- Digital files are tagged, dates are corrected

- Slides and negatives are scanned at 4000 DPI

- Videos and film are remastered, saved as AVI or MOV

- Back-up includes two digital copies, one onsite (off the main computer) and one offsite

We are committed to educating consumers and our clients on what standards will best preserve their memories for the future. However, these levels of service do come at a higher price point.

When we find that clients are looking for a lower cost solution, we offer Consumer Level services as well, but it is not our recommended level of service. However, if photos are being preserved at this level, it is better than not at all.

Consumer Level – Common Practices – Many times, people access consumer levels of services because they are unaware there are other options and considerations to ensure their photos and family movies will be around for generations to come. Some consumers do choose to have a lower cost service and are willing to compromise on the quality of service. Some of these services consumers can do themselves at home.

- Photos are scanned on flatbed scanners with unknown DPI and quality
- Digital files are saved on DVDs, jump drives with no consideration of how the photo will be organized and found later
- Slides and negatives are scanned using a consumer grade scanner with inconsistent color correction
- Videos and film are transferred to lower size and quality digital formats (MP4s or MPGs) or transferred and compressed straight to a DVD

APPENDIX D – YOUR PHOTO INVENTORY

Imagine bringing all your photos together in one place so you can do something with them!

Check which of these materials you have in your photo collection. Circle the items that you'd like to work on in the next few months.

☐ Printed photos	☐ Audios
☐ Photo albums	☐ Film
☐ Boxes of photos	☐ Memorabilia
☐ Misc. loose photos	☐ Important family documents
☐ Framed photos	
☐ Slides	☐ Genealogical records
☐ Negatives	☐ Other (list)
☐ Digital Photos	_______________________
☐ Videos	

Now, imagine your photos were gone tomorrow. Weather, time and technology failures are waiting to steal your memories and family legacy away.

We are here to help you!

APPENDIX E – RESOURCES

Pixologie

www.pixologieinc.com

Telephone: 414-731-1881

Email: mollieb@pixologieinc.com

Click on the Tools Link for free downloads, worksheets and more. Purchase Flip Pal Scanners, Legacy Boxes and other tools.

E-Z Photo Scan

www.ezphotoscan.com

Telephone: 866-562-4660

Email: info@ezphotoscan.com

Kodak Alaris Picture Saver System Scanning Rentals

FOREVER®

www.forever.com

Products including permanent photo storage, photobook software and much more. Please select Pixologie, Oak Creek, WI as we'd love to be your ambassador and be connected to you. We do receive a commission on sales

Mollie Bartelt, photo estate planner, Pixologist, mission-driven entrepreneur, is on a mission to save people's stories and ensure future generations have a meaningful photographic family history.

Mollie's career started in the nonprofit, healthcare and assisted living fields, where she ran adult day centers and other community programs to help older adults remain living in the community. Even back then, she saw the value of family photographs and photo albums as a comfort and memory tool for her clients.

Quitting her healthcare career in 2014, Mollie and her friend, Ann Matuszak opened Pixologie's first location. She works with clients individually, teaches photo organization classes and has helped organize over one million photos since starting.

Mollie is married to Paul and has two children, Hannah and Alexander. She sings in her church choir and her goal is to help make the world a better place by helping people enjoy and share their memories and family histories.

Available at Amazon.com

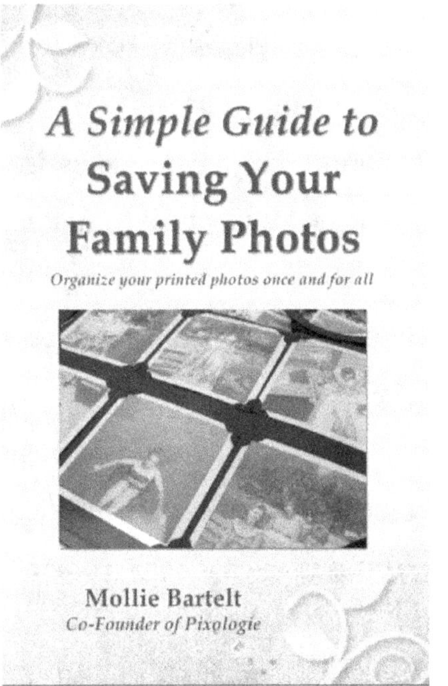

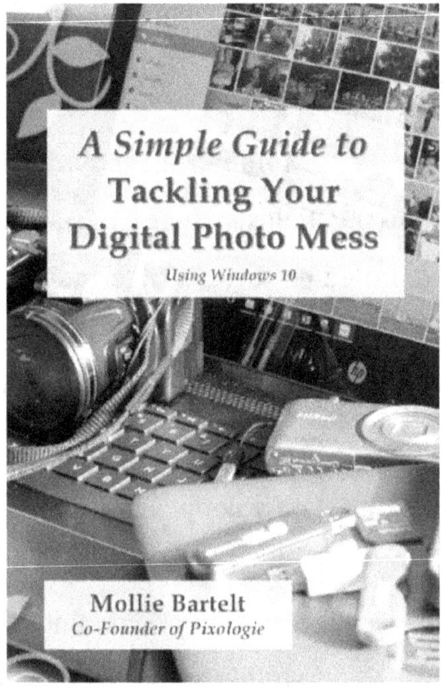

~ NOTES ~

~ NOTES ~

~ NOTES ~

98

~ NOTES ~

~ NOTES ~